I CHANGED MY MIND

It's Not What You Think

EBONI KING

authorHOUSE®

AuthorHouse™
1663 Liberty Drive
Bloomington, IN 47403
www.authorhouse.com
Phone: 833-262-8899

Published by AuthorHouse   05/25/2021

ISBN: 978-1-5246-0413-4 (sc)
ISBN: 978-1-5246-0416-5 (e)

Print information available on the last page.

Any people depicted in stock imagery provided by Thinkstock are models, and such images are being used for illustrative purposes only. Certain stock imagery © Thinkstock.

This book is printed on acid-free paper.

Scripture quotations marked NIV are taken from the Holy Bible, New International Version®. NIV®. Copyright © 1973, 1978, 1984 by International Bible Society. Used by permission of Zondervan. All rights reserved. [Biblica

Scripture quotations marked NLT are taken from the Holy Bible, New Living Translation, copyright © 1996, 2004, 2007. Used by permission of Tyndale House Publishers, Inc. Carol Stream, Illinois 60188. All rights reserved. Website

Unless otherwise indicated, all scripture quotations are from The Holy Bible, English Standard Version® (ESV®). Copyright ©2001 by Crossway Bibles, a division of Good News Publishers. Used by permission. All rights reserved.

CONTENTS

You must have the same attitude that Christ
Jesus had. —Philippians 2:5 NIV

THIRTY-NINE QUOTES

1. You cannot write about bondage and walk in freedom.
2. When your mouth speaks of freedom, your mind will agree.
3. However you see yourself, so too will others.
4. As you release yourself from people's opinions, you can grab hold of more opportunities.
5. Sow today what you want to reap tomorrow.
6. You cannot make up for lost time; you can use the time you have now wisely.
7. Have you ever wondered, "Where did time go?" Nowhere. It just doesn't stand still.
8. Every day is a gift for you to unwrap.
9. Give what you think you don't have, and receive what you didn't know you needed.
10. Everything is not always as it seems, but it will be what you think.
11. Think right, and you'll speak right.
12. Don't say in this minute what you don't want to take back in the next hour.
13. One hour is sixty minutes. But it only takes a second to say something you'll regret forever.
14. Regrets are things done or said without meaning.
15. Meaningless things are done without precaution.
16. Caution taken doesn't mean you're scared. It means you're careful.
17. Be careful who you tell where you're going. They might get there before you.
18. Competition is a silent prejudice.
19. Prejudice often acts before it speaks.
20. Wrong perception often leads to a wrong conception.
21. Seek firsthand knowledge.
22. Secondhand information about a person is words without knowledge.
23. God is the only one who has unlimited knowledge.
24. Seek him along your journey and get there on purpose.
25. A purpose-filled life is a life at the right speed.

26. Fulfilling your purpose has nothing to do with age.
27. If you have breath, the sky is still within your reach.
28. If you still have hope, you are still in the lane on your way to your destination.
29. Landing at a crossroad doesn't mean a dead end.
30. This is the place where you make your flight decision.
31. Your landing is always smoother than takeoff.
32. Remember where you were, but seize your time here.
33. A misstep doesn't always mean you have failed. It means you have learned to take bigger steps.
34. In order to step into destiny, you have to come through history.
35. Faith got you going, and it will keep you moving.
36. What you see now you weren't ready for then.
37. Preparation is like a steering wheel in a car.
38. Process is what a pilot is to a plane. You can't take off without it.
39. Let living on purpose be your highest pursuit!

But remember the Lord your God for It Is He Who Gives you the ability to produce wealth, and so confirm His covenants, Which He swore to your forefathers, As It Is today.

Entrust your efforts to the Lord, and your planning will succeed (Proverbs 16:3).

SUCCESS

Substantial
Usage
Coming
Constantly
Effecting
Society
Successfully

SUCCESS QUOTES

1. Success is empowerment.

2. Success is an opportunity to propel yourself into alignment with God's grace. That will enable you to operate effectively (uniquely) in the gifts and talents he has bestowed upon you. You are gifted!

3. Success truly starts when believers capture their identity in Christ.

4. Success requires relationships with people who have the same mind-set and are working toward the same goal.

5. Can two people walk together without agreeing on the direction? Do two walk together unless they have agreed to do so?

6. Success is learning that your presence is more valuable than any gift. Presence is the gift enhancer.

7. Success has an enemy, which is fear. The friend of success is faith.

8. Success in essence is fulfilling the assignment on your life that God has marked with his fingerprint.

9. Success must be seen in your mind before you can achieve it with your hand.

10. Success cannot be accessed by a feeling. Believe and begin. Achievement awaits you!

11. Success is not determined by who doesn't believe in you. You must believe in yourself.

12. Success begins with a planted seed. Start with what you have.

13. Success involves doors, closed and opened. Either way, it requires you to walk out in order to walk in. God is your door controller.

14. Success is often staring at you while you are looking for it. Look within.

15. Success in its fullest expression is walking out of the ordinary into the extraordinary. You are peculiar!

16. Success from God often comes dressed as opposition. Just keep pushing; it will unveil itself as your opportunity. You are successful!

17. Success in God's eyes is not as we see with our natural eyes. Let faith be your vision.

18. Success rewards are in the things that take the least amount of effort.

19. Success from heaven will anoint your head and allow your oil to flow indoors and outdoors. You are prosperous!

20. Success from God is packaged in selflessness, which allows him
    to make you a deliverer of blessings.

21. Success is being empowered with the education needed to influence the environment in which you are stationed. Get involved.

22. Success is not a product. It's a person: you!

23. Success is not an event. It's an attitude.

24. Success is a movement. Act now!

25. Success is a doorway to your destiny. Enter in!

26. Success requires patience under saturated hands. Push! Pray until success happens.

27. Success is activated with four spoken words. Use your own mouth. You can do this!

28. Success is more rewarding with knowledge of and wisdom from God and self.

29. Success begins when you start and ends when you finish. Start again! Love by faith.

30. Success should be founded on love. Any field you take with love as the leader, you are qualified.

OPINIONS

Other's
Peoples
Incomplete
News
Ideas
Outbursts
Negatives
Sometimes

LOVE

Live
Out
Victory
Everyday

Faith is not meant to be understood. It's meant to be excepted beyond the natural. In order to tap into the supernatural where God dwells. That's the realm where you walk in accordance with the will of God despite the natural realm contradictions. You see, hear, and say what God says. Walk In Faith. Faith assures us of things we expect and convinces us of the existence of things we cannot see (Hebrews 11:1).

Do everything in love (1 Corinthians 16:14).

Pursue love, and desire spiritual gifts, but especially the gift of speaking what God has revealed (1 Corinthians 14:1).

Now eagerly desire the greater gifts, and yet I will show you the most excellent way (1 Corinthians 12:1).

You will succeed in whatever you choose to do, and light will shine on the road ahead of you (Job 22:28).

It's impossible to be taken in by God, who is love, and be infected with his love and not spread it to others.

If you believe, you will receive whatever you ask for in prayer (Matthew 21:22 NLT).

You can pray for anything, and if you have faith, you will receive it.

Know this: God is Lord. He made us; we didn't make him. We're his people, his well-timed sheep that enter with this password: *Thank you!* Make yourselves at home, give him praise, thank him, and worship him, for God is sheer beauty, generous in love, and loyal always and ever.

Commit your way to the Lord; trust in him, and he will do this (Psalm 37:8).

If you are not firm in faith, you will not be firm at all (Isaiah 7:9 ESV).

If you don't remain faithful, you won't remain standing (Isaiah 7:9).

If you don't take your stand in faith, you won't have a leg to stand on.

Faithful is he who calls you, and he also will do it (1 Thessalonians 5:24).

This people I have formed for myself; they shall show forth my praise (Isaiah 43:21).

Point your kids in the right direction; when they're old, they won't be lost (Proverbs 22:4).

The Lord is righteous; he loves justice, and the upright will see his face (Psalm 11:7).

You cause me to know the path of life. In your presence is joyful abundance; at your right hand there are pleasures forever (Psalm 16:11).

May the Lord lead your hearts into a full understanding and expression of the love of God and the patient endurance that comes from Christ.

Now you've got my feet on the life path, all radiant from the shining of your face. Ever since you took my hand, I'm on the right way (Psalm 16:11).

It's what we trust in but don't yet see that keeps us going.

Indeed our lives are guided by faith, not by sight (2 Corinthians 5:7).

LOVE BY FAITH

Love
Only
Validates
Effort
Basically
Your
Faith
Actually
Initiated
Through
Heaven

The Lord was talking to me about unconditional love. He loved us in our worst state. We had nothing of any value to offer him when Jesus came to redeem us to our original state. Now the only way to receive his love, which is an unconditional love that took all the conditions we had (and I do mean "had"), is the exchange of our life for his. With him we have no conditions for which he had to answer. He took our inability to believe and gave us love by faith. What a love walk! Love, live, give, and receive, all by faith! Amen.

"Your love for one another will prove to the world that you are my disciples" (John 13:35 NLT).

Growing up wasn't always pleasant. I saw and heard a lot. I was surrounded by people under the influence of drugs. I was so terrified that something bad was going to happen. I remember praying to God, not knowing if he was there or listening. I was about six years old.

There were times when I was awoken from the screaming and hollering. I believed that I would die. It had to be a miracle that we all survived.

A man ran with one of the biggest gangsters, who is now deceased. He was a veteran. His mind was corrupted. I remember being awoken at midnight on Christmas Eve. Instead of wanting to open a present, I was looking at the story about Jesus of Nazareth, saying, "Please help." Through all that, I could still love. He was still, in my eyes, the greatest man in the world. I was considered the most favored by him.

Years later I tried to sell drugs for a dealer. Once I took my money off the top, I took it back to him and told him I was done. He said "No, you have to sell it all. Where is the rest?"

I told him, "I spent it."

He said, "Baby girl, that's not the way it goes." And he laughed, and I laughed.

It's funny what laughter can do. He could have hurt me or had me hurt. Instead he let it go.

The funny part about this story is that some years later, I ended up becoming well off in that field myself. I saw the guy again. This time he was coming to me for help. I had not forgotten what he did years before. It's funny that I was the only one to whom he came to that didn't turn him down. Years later he ended up back at the top again, as they call it. He came looking for me to become his business partner. I did. That was successful for a little while. He is now deceased.

I thank God that he had a plan for my life. I wasn't even aware of it at the time. I always felt in my heart that church was the answer. Now I know that Christ is the answer. Church is where you go to celebrate the answer.

One day I said to one of my workers, "Let's go to church," and she said, "Okay." I remembered a church that my friend attended. We headed over there, and upon entering, we felt so unwelcome. After leaving, we felt worse than we did when we came in. It's sad how that same problem still exists in some churches.

Now I understand why her life never changed for the better. She is now deceased. I believe that's why my friend's brother had a hard time going to church. He had watched his sister go and had seen no evidence of change. He had witnessed his mother be abused by men. I believe he was very bitter and angry at God after watching his mom, whom he loved more than anything, die at a young age. A few years later he watched his sister pass away from cancer. I believe the misery from his childhood caused him to be abusive and addicted to sex. He was trying to bury his pain.

I should have known that without Christ in both of our lives, we were headed for destruction. I think we often get caught up in the moment. There's a song by Shirley Murdock called "As We Lay." There is so much in that song that can help you not make a wreck of your life. I like this verse: "We forgot about the price we had to pay ... We should have counted up the cost but instead we got lost in the second, in the minute, in the hour as we lay." Often the enemy blinds us from what a decision will cost us. I think about myself and how certain decisions in my life cost me.

I found out that everyone in this life will have a valley encounter. It is there that you can learn to trust God. Learn that he is God and that you are his. I've always heard the saying, "He will never leave you nor forsake you." I've found that we have the free will to walk away from him. You won't know what you're made of if God doesn't let you go through the storm. You can rest assured that if you trust God, you will come out with power. I learned a lot about myself in the valley. I learned that people are just people. They will let you down all the time—sometimes intentionally and other times because they can't help it.

God wants you to hold onto the horns of the altar. Your strength will enable you to keep moving forward when others are trying to stop you. Your pressing on excites the heart of God. He is observing you. He also is observing the satanic and orchestrated effort to stop you, discourage you, distract you, and disappoint you. He knows how hard you have to fight your way through to get into your future. God is not stupid. He already has spotted your enemies—your untrue friends, your undiscerning family members who cannot sense the divine destiny driving you straight into your diving future, an almost unbelievable assignment.

Your strength will stop you from crumbling when the rushing waves of anger from others storm your beliefs and persuasions. You know what you believe. God has appointed you, anointed you, chosen you, and declared to his angels his personal plans for your life. He has already decided to side with you and to demonstrate his divine favor toward you. It is already settled in the heart of God. You will obtain the promise, the blessing, the divine destiny he predestined for you. But you must decide to be strong for his plan to be completed. His plan *requires* your personal decision to be strong.

Your strength will demoralize and discourage those who have purposed to change your focus, divert your energy, and stop your momentum. Your life is moving very, very fast toward the center of your divine assignment. Swifter in the spirit world than your own mind is comprehending, and it is shocking the demons assigned to stop you. They feel powerless to slow you down. The demons assigned to stop you feel powerless to slow you down. You have an adversary that you have not seen, a different enemy from what you have identified, but your strength is a demoralizing factor in his planning session. Your enemy is losing confidence. God wants you to know this.

Your strength is choking the enemy. Your strength is torturous to the seducing Delilah Spirit that was hired to break you, crush you, stop you, and halt your momentum, just as the philistine Lords paid to set up Sampson. The enemy has tried to set up bait to lure you, bring you into a stupor or slumber, a false sense of rest, but the warring spirit inside of you, stood up, fought back, and refused to lie down. God doesn't want you to be like anybody else. Your difference may anger others, but it's a good thing. You truly are a warrior, and it is your strength that the supernatural God ordained that is rising up again to take hold of the divine mandate of God, the divine message of your life. He will use your mess and turn it into your message, your appointed legacy, the invisible promise that has gripped your soul since childhood.

Your strength will enable you to give proper birth to the vision God had of your life when he formed you. A mother pregnant with her child requires the strength to carry the child full term. The baby can be perfectly formed, complete and whole. If she is not healthy, the birth can be premature, the fetus can be aborted, or the baby can be stillborn. A dead child brings years of sorrow, and it can bring a spirit of death into the marriage of a young couple. There is no greater blow to a young marriage. It strips the countenance of expectations, ecstasy, and enthusiasm. It tears hope into shreds. That's why you must be strong. You must give birth to the baby, the calling of God. You must fight with every ounce within you to gain strength.

Your strength is your personal decision and requires all your attention and focus at this time in your life. Nobody can decide this for you. Move toward it now. Unclutter the relationships entangling your emotions and thoughts. Ruthlessly swipe away the webs that the spiders have weaved around your mind.

God is ready to do new things. Believe it. Keep this in your spirit: "I have no choice but to trust him. That's all I can do. I have no other choice but to believe. Say that's what I will do" (Isaiah 43). The message is: *You're my handpicked servant. Come to know and trust me, understand both that I am and who I am. Previous to me there was no such thing as a God, nor will there be after me. I—yes, I—am God. I'm the only Savior there is. I spoke, I saved, and I told you what existed long before these upstart gods appeared on the scene. And you know it. You're my witnesses. You're the evidence.*

Yes, I am God. I've always been God, and I always will be God. No one can take anything from me. I make; who can unmake it?

Behold, I will do a new thing. Now it shall spring forth. Shall you not know it? I will even make a way in the wilderness. I will erase every past desert of disappointment. I will restore your personal faith. There will even be rivers in your desert. God is moving swifter than you ever imagined to catapult you into your Canaan, land of hope and promise. This is a personal word of hope. God is restoring the joy of salvation. Get ready. Your time has come. The dream is for the appointed time, and your appointed time has come. In the end it shall speak and not lie. Wait for it, because it will surely come. It will not tarry!

And it's impossible to please God without faith, and anyone who wants to come to him must believe that he exists and that he rewards those who sincerely seek him (Hebrews 11:6).

Journal

Journal

_____
_____
_____
_____
_____
_____
_____
_____
_____
_____
_____
_____
_____
_____
_____
_____
_____
_____
_____
_____
_____
_____
_____
_____
_____
_____
_____
_____
_____
_____
_____

Journal

Journal

Journal

I'm not guilty, and you're not guilty. I have been living a life pleasing unto God for more than ten years. I have learned the love of Christ for myself. I've learned to walk in the freedom of life given through Christ on the cross. What a relief this has been to no longer live that way. The power of God allows you to flee anything that's contrary to his word. If the Son sets you free, you are free indeed. Why is it that the thought of things we used to do seem to have an effect on us more now than they did when we used to do them?

Here is your answer: guilt. Guilt is a feeling of responsibility for wrongdoing. "Feeling" is a key word. Feelings can lead you the wrong way if not governed properly. A lot of people are suffering from guilt, and this has affected many families and relationships, including one of the most important relationships that you can ever have in this life: that with God the Father. Guilt can be a life-stealing disease. There is an unseen force behind this, which is the devil himself. He is the invisible disease. He enters your mind or uses people to plant things in your mind. He will hunt you with something from your past.

I used to be the queen of sin (you could have called me Las Vegas), because I was walking in darkness. I knew no light (the word of God). However, I started early and grew up quickly. I had children at an early age (by different men) and abortions, I was a hustler—you name it, that was me. I didn't steal or use drugs. I never willingly had sexual relationships with women. You're probably wondering why I said "willingly." Well, you may need to be free from thinking you're guilty because your innocence was taken from you, whether be by male or female. You might think you must subject yourself to that guilt. And maybe because of that, this has caused you to be in a same-sex relationship. Or caused you to wonder if you're supposed to be in that kind of relationship. But you know deep down in your heart that this kind of relationship was not intended. Neither with a different gender nor outside of marriage.

Journal

Journal

Journal

Journal

_____
_____
_____
_____
_____
_____
_____
_____
_____
_____
_____
_____
_____
_____
_____
_____
_____
_____
_____
_____
_____
_____
_____
_____
_____
_____
_____
_____

I was about as innocent as I can remember, around eight years old, and living in the projects when a twelve- or thirteen-year-old girl wanted to have oral sex with me. Now that I think about it, this must have been done to her by someone in her family or by someone close to her. I don't know how it came about, but I became a victim of her nightmare. Nobody suspected anything like that could be happening, but it was. I was too afraid to say anything.

It didn't carry on long. There was a party at the center in the neighborhood, and a shooting broke out. The girl was shot and killed. Believe it or not, I was really sad. In spite of her taking my innocence, I loved her as a friend and a big sister. For some reason I didn't ask to go to the funeral.

If you were a victim of this kind of sexual impurity, you are free from guilt, in the name of Jesus. If this kind of sexual activity has been performed on you unwillingly, you are free to receive your healing and deliverance, in the name of Jesus. Forgive yourself. Then forgive that person. I declare that you are free, by the power of the blood of Jesus.

I thank God that I didn't allow that experience to cause me to pursue same-sex relationships, because that's what the enemy intended. So if you have entered into abnormal relationships because of your past and want to come out, you can, in the name of Jesus. The enemy didn't succeed with confusing me with women, but he got me with men.

I ended up having sex at a very young age. I got pregnant. Then I got pregnant again and had my second child at the age of fifteen. By this time I had grown up so quickly that I started to believe I was older than I was.

I surrounded myself with people older than me. I acted more mature than they did. Then I moved on to the next relationship. By that time I had turned sixteen but felt about twenty-three in my mind. I was moving from one unhealthy relationship to another. I became a magnet for these kinds of relationships. I was in mental bondage because of what had happened to me. I was a victim of guilt, hurt, shame, and defeat. I didn't know what to do to get out. This began to seem like a normal lifestyle. I thought I would never see anything different. When I met Jesus and got to know him for myself, he let me know that I could now repent, for the kingdom of heaven was at hand. What this meant to me was that heaven was there to help me.

I began to pursue the Lord and Savior for myself. That's exactly what I needed him to be, and that is what you should do if you want to see change in your life.

You may be wondering where my family was in all this. So I'm going to give you a little information. By the time I had my second child, I had become so mature that I believed that everybody forgot how old I was. I did. Now don't judge my family, because even though they were not present, they were the best family I could have had. God doesn't make mistakes. He chooses your family. It's just that sometimes they don't choose rightly. My father died when I was sixteen, and I was devastated. I felt so guilty that I wanted to die.

The Lord cares deeply when his loved ones dies (Psalm 116:15 NLT).

In the sight of the Lord, the death of his faithful ones is valued (Psalm 116:15 ISV).

My father loved me, and I loved him. He was my heart. He did all he could to protect me. When I first became pregnant and he found out (I hid it for about five months), he was so hurt. He probably felt guilty. I'm sure he didn't understand when and where I got pregnant. And how could a child of his, at thirteen years of age, even be thinking about sex? My parents never talked about sex around us (worst mistake). It's important to talk to your children about sex (not the birds and the bees). I thought my whole world had come to an end when he suddenly died after I thought he was getting better, although we had signs that death could be near.

I never thought that this could happen to me—not at this age. Since then, God has graced me with wisdom and understanding about death. When that happened I felt guilty and wanted to disappear. I just wanted to go to sleep, wake up, and realize this was all a nightmare. How I wish I could've told him one last time how much I loved him. The song "Dance with My Father" by Luther Vandross is so dear to my heart. I soon had to learn that I wasn't having a nightmare, that this was real life happening to real people.

In his hand is the life of every creature and the breath of all mankind (Job 12:10).

Don't you know he enjoys giving rest to those he loves (Psalm 127:2)?

My ex's mother died a day before my father died, and that was even more painful. She and I were very close. I was expecting again at the time of both their departures. My goodness, he probably would have passed out or something had he known.

After those two devastating deaths, I immediately became a full-time street hustler. I became so well-off that I was able to hire people. I began to live a dangerous lifestyle. I'm so glad the Lord had a plan for my life even though I didn't know it at the time. He says it like this: "I know the thoughts that I think toward you, thoughts of peace, and not of evil, to give you an expected end" (Jeremiah 29:11). I'm so glad that the Lord's thoughts toward me were good back then. I didn't think good of myself. I'm so glad the Lord sees not how you are but how you can become in him. I stand on if any man or woman be in Christ he is a new creature and that old things are past and (passing) away and are becoming new. Depending on how far you went before you accepted Christ's invitation, this particular message could mean a lot to you once it takes root. It will become a revelation in your spirit and take hold of your soul. You will value walking in newness and feeling the joy of it.

You can come to know the living word while walking in daily fellowship with the Father, Son, and the Holy Spirit. I can testify to the scripture that states the one who is forgiven is much loved. I have been forgiven of much. I love Jesus. He has helped me to love humanity. The Lord has loved me unconditionally in spite of my shortcomings. I can see what God saw when he died for us while we were sinners. The word says that love covers a multitude of sins. That's what Jesus was on that cross; he was our covering. I will be forever grateful for his love. I will do my best to please him eternally.

The body is not for sexual immorality but for the Lord. Outside a covenant with the Lord, I was used as an experiment. In fact, this is what sex outside of marriage is: an experiment (a controlled procedure carried out to discover, test, or demonstrate something). My body had become an experiment, and that can be mentally abusive by itself, no matter what age you are. It can be even more devastating depending upon the age of the person.

My innocence was stolen. Once you experience something that is too mature for you, your body responds accordingly, and your actions follow. This is why once teenagers and young adults become physically or sexually involved with others, they begin to act differently. They become aware before their time. Premature exposure can cause a lot of damage. It takes a whole new bloodline to restore what was lost. That's what Jesus did for me. At my advice, my ex left and remarried. Now, all the women, all the baby mamas, are no longer my breakfast, lunch, or dinner. My mind has been at peace with that relationship. The enemy wanted me to be mentally lost, but now we are friends, by the grace of God. I have now been living a celibate life for almost 10 years. I'm happy with myself. I have more joy than I've ever had before.

God said, "You had a husband. I'm giving you a marriage."

Making
Arrangements
Right
Respectfully
Including
Almighty
God
Every day

The joy of the Lord has been my strength through all of this. I will continue to wait on the Lord for my marriage. I vow not to have sex until I go to the altar and say, "I will."

Now I'm beginning to understand what Jesus meant when he said you are made whole (physically and spiritually). One cannot be successful without the other. I think about so much that is going on with people around the world and how people have become so open with a lot of things that used to be considered shameful. I think about people crying out for help. I think about women caught in adultery. Maybe these women want to get caught. Maybe they have been victims themselves. Maybe they are trying to inflict pain rather than being hurt. Neither one is right. And the script doesn't say who the married one was. It just states the condition. But I find it strange that she was the only one who they thought needed to be brought to Jesus. In fact, they both should have been brought to Jesus. I think for far too long women have been misjudged and called everything but children of God. Women, men, and children need to know their value.

One New Year's Day I decided to go to the movies with a friend of mine. I happened to run into a boyfriend whom I hadn't seen in about a week, and he was not alone. My friend spotted him, and I went after him. He and the two women with him left the show. I immediately jumped in my car and tried to find them. I drove about 100 mph on the expressway. I could have killed myself. I couldn't find them, and I thought to myself, *This is it. I can't take any more of his behavior.* I was crying out for help. I decided to do what he was doing. I started dating a guy in the neighborhood. I was hoping he would catch me and leave me alone. And thanks to one of his friends, he did catch me. He was brought where I was. I was sitting in the car with my friend, whom I had come to care about deeply. He treated me like a lady. He approached the car, and his behavior was outrageous. It was almost as if he had forgotten about what he had just done and had been doing for quite some time.

He was not bold enough to put his hands on me with all those people out there. The police had arrived, as well. He spit in my face and said, "You nasty B. How could you be down here with him?" Whenever I think about this, I think about how Jesus felt when they spit on him and abused him when he left eternity to come and save us. Remember that it's still your choice where you want your soul to live.

I needed to get out. Finally, by the grace of God, I did. Even though it didn't end after that, there was a divine exit of that episode in my life, and another one to come. I didn't get it until I allowed God to intervene in my life. It's funny that a man can sleep with different women, and people laugh it off and call him a player, but if a woman sleeps with different men, she's called a whore. Both the men and the women have not learned the value of sex and have not come to the revelation that sex is designed for marriage. A man and a woman choose to give their hearts and then their bodies to one another as something sacred after marriage. Men and women both have to learn this. When they brought the woman to Jesus and didn't bother to bring the man, the scripture says Jesus stooped down and wrote on the ground with his finger, as though he did not hear (John 8:6). I believe he wrote, "Not guilty," because he had come to fulfill the law and give us freedom in him.

John 8:7 says, "When they continued asking him he raised himself up and said to them, 'He who is without sin among you, let him throw a stone at her first."

John 8:8 says again he stooped down and wrote on the ground. I believe this time he wrote, "Where is the man?" At that very moment, one of the acts of darkness had come into the face of the light and life for mankind. They both needed forgiveness, love, and freedom in Christ.

When the Lord delivered me from my sinful ways, I wanted to let everyone know that I had sinned. That same power is still available today. The Bible says—and I can testify—Jesus is the same "today, yesterday, and forever." He does not change. That same power is available to you, and it will be available whenever you need it. If you need to call on him, do that. He said, "Whosoever shall call on the name of the Lord shall be saved."

The Bible doesn't say women or men have fallen short. It says, "We all have come short of the glory of God." Jesus was sent, because we all need him to reach God's height. Apart from him we are all guilty. With him we are not guilty. Jesus took the punishment. His blood paid the penalty. So every time the devil accuses us if we have accepted his sacrificial life and his eternal blood. Then he is indeed Lord and Savior of your life. God then looks at us, sees Jesus, and says, "Not guilty." We no longer have to be shameful. We can say with joy and boldness in the Holy Ghost, "I was once blind, and now I see."

I say with gladness that who the Son set free is free indeed. Walk in that freedom every day of your life. You have victory over drug addiction, sexual immorality, prostitution, adultery, low self-esteem, and all other kinds of spirits. Jesus has already paid for your victory over everything to which the enemy would try to keep you in bondage. Any man in Christ is a new creature. Anytime you want something new, you have to be willing to change something. The best thing about change is that if there is no wrong, then there's no room for right. Evil despises right. What people don't understand is that you can be religious or spiritual, but that alone will not bring about a change. The lack of knowledge of whom Jesus Christ is and whom he is to you personally makes the difference.

This is exactly why Jesus asked Peter, "Who do men say that I am?"

Then Peter confessed, "Christ the son of the living God."

Jesus replied, "This was not revealed to you by man but by my father in heaven."

That very moment he knew Jesus's identity. This is why the Bible says, "You will overcome him by the blood of the lamb and by the word of your own testimony"—not Grandma's, not Mama's, not Pastor's, not anyone else's. You must have this testimony for yourself. This is how you can stay in the race. Once you become free, then you begin to change. You see differently, and your world begins to change. Then you begin to experience newness. You're on your way to wholeness. Everybody's process is different, depending upon where you came from.

Let's take the woman at the well. We know that she already had a place to worship and had some idea of how things should be. Still she had no peace. John 4:7 says, "There cometh a woman of Samaria to draw water," and Jesus said unto her, 'Give me a drink.'"

John 4:8 says, "For his disciples were gone away to buy meat."

John 4:9 says, "The woman says unto him, 'How is it that thou, be a Jew askest drink of me which am a woman of Samaria?'" Jews had no dealings with the Samaritans.

Let's pause here for a moment and concentrate on these three verses. In between the conversation, the text tells us that his disciples went away to buy meat, which means this conversation was between Jesus and the woman at the well. We all know that Jesus is going to be Jesus.

Let me zero in on a situation that I recently encountered. People quite often misunderstand what Jesus said. For example, in John 4:31–34, he was speaking of meat and his disciples were quarreling over who brought him food. Remember that they walked with him and still didn't get him. Everyone will not understand you.

Now let's look at this from today's view. The woman said "Jews," so she must has been referring to a nationality or gender. They must not have had any dealings with the women except physical relations. Jesus knows this already. He has chosen to meet her. Without the other men that don't deal with women on a spiritual level. He doesn't even waste his breath talking about it. Some things are just meant to be ignored.

He replies by saying, "If thou newest the gift of God and who it is that said to thee, give me to drink; thou would have ask of him, and he would have giving thee living water." In other words, we should expect controversy whenever women reach their destiny by having encounters with Jesus. Women begin to display their knowledge of Jesus as their Lord and Savior. If you think about all the division that the enemy has caused regarding women speaking in the church, no wonder there is so much estrangement before they succeed as husband and wife. I thought that it wasn't man alone but through the empowerment of the Holy Spirit that he enables his work to be done. If that's the case, what is all the fighting and competition about? When the enemy gets involved, his duty is to keep men and women from reaching that intimate place with God. This can be established through the reading of his word, prayer, and worship. The enemy plans will crumble. You're no longer depending on man alone. You're looking to God. Then once you begin to reach for him, you see that he has been reaching for you all the time. Once you realize that, you won't be as distracted by searching for something to satisfy your flesh, which can be satisfied only by God himself.

John 4:18 says you have had five husbands, and the man you are now living with is not your husband. He could be saying that even though you live with him, he is not the man who you are supposed to marry, which would have made him husband number six. You should spend time in the presence of the Lord if you have found yourself in this very situation. Allow him to speak to you through his word so that you may know which way to go.

The woman says to him, "Sir, I see and understand that you are a prophet." This is where the enemy will be glad to keep you—in a state where you're always looking for a word from someone else. Oftentimes God wants to speak to you first or show you (Jeremiah 33:3). Some things will be for your ears and your ears only. I'm not saying that receiving a word from God by way of his messenger is not valid. I am saying that you can't live that way. At some point you may have to deliver a word. The gift comes from God. When it's your time to give, if you have been spending quality time with God, you're ready. Go to the Bible with this in mind:

Believe
In
Better
Living
Every day

God says, "I will pour out my spirit on all people." Your sons and daughters will prophesy, your young men will see visions, and your old men will dream. Even on my servants, both men and women, I will pour out my spirit, and they will prophesy, and all this will take place before the coming of the great and glorious day of the Lord. I believe that we are in the last hour. Jesus will be returning soon. Until that day you can call on the righteous name of the Lord.

This is the way you become familiar with his voice and he becomes familiar with yours. You may be the only person who someone will be willing to listen to. When you receive a gift, it's common to check the tag to see who the sender is. The enemy assignment is to make sure you can't answer when somebody asks you where you get your joy, peace, salvation, and so forth—that you can't say Jesus! His name has the power to distribute everything he promised.

It doesn't come from knowing your pastor. It doesn't come because your husband or wife is a pastor. It doesn't come from friendship or membership. Salvation comes through faith in Jesus Christ. The enemy wants to keep you from fully developing. I remember carrying my first child. I was bearing at a very young age. My cervix would not open up sufficiently to deliver the baby the natural way. I had to have a C-section. The doctor had to cut me, which is what the devil tries to do to us when we have not reached the highest level that God wants us to be in him. God knows what it takes, and when he has tried us, we shall come forth as pure gold (Isaiah 10:27). If we get sidetracked, then we will end up with scrapes and bruises. Like the women with the five husbands, it will be a waste of your and their time. If you truly belong to God, anything that's not his will, will never last.

"I know the Messiah cometh, which is called Christ; when he is come, he will tell us all things" (John 4:25).

"Jesus said unto her, I that speak unto thee am He" (John 4:26).

"The woman then left her water pot and went her way into the city and said unto the men" (John 4:28).

"She replied, 'Come see a man, which told me all things that ever I did; is not this the Christ.' Selah!" (John 4:29).

The text says the woman left her water pot and went and told the men to come see a man who told me all things. This special encounter she had with Jesus changed her thinking. She needed a man. Now she was sharing the good news about Christ, something that apparently she had not done before. Get ready to do something that has never been done! It reminds me of a scripture that says, "Eye have not seen nor have Ears heard the things which God has in store for them that love him." That's very personal to me. It means your best is yet to come.

John 4:39 says, "Many of the Samaritans of that city believed in him because of that saying of the woman, which testified, he told me all that I ever did." This is one of the most important verses. When the enemy came and tried to cripple her ministry by making her fearful of her past, Jesus cleared the way. God doesn't always call the qualified. However, he qualifies those whom he calls. Don't let your past hinder you. Let it be the very thing that helps push you forward. Remind yourself daily that somebody somewhere can benefit from something that you overcame.

God works for the good in all things. I had numerous supernatural encounters with Jesus. My life hasn't been the same since. It didn't stop there. Thank you, Jesus!

In order to experience these divine visitations, you have to be thirsty. This means that you have to want to be free. You can be a prisoner and not even be in jail. For example, you can be a slave to something you want to get out of.

Now let's consider the movie *The Color Purple*. Whoopi Goldberg played a child with low self-esteem. She was raped by her father, who turned out not to be her real father. She conceived two children. After being forced out of her house and into a marriage that she did not want, she had to raise his children while being mentally and physically abused. At one point she couldn't read. This movie was very inspirational to me. While learning to read, she was constantly talking and writing to God. She didn't even know he was listening. Ms. Celie was faithful during the time she was there and being abused. The Lord was making sure that in the end everything would turn around for the good.

Faithfulness is a key factor. It pays off spiritually. In the beginning, the enemy attacks you hard. In the middle the pain slackens. Toward your exit he comes harder. By then your walk with Christ should be stronger. Then you are on your way to a glorious victory! Finally, you have found out how awesome God truly is. All the glory belongs to God!

In my wilderness experience, I had to fight my way through like Oprah in *The Color Purple*. This fight was like being in the movies *Chucky, Nightmare on Elm Street,* and *Jason.* It was like I had a hit out on me, but because of the standard of the Lord, I was never killed. I have work to do, and so do you. At this place in my life the Lord began to hide me under the shadow of his wings. Where his blood is applied, no devil can come. Anything that doesn't have the blood on it and tries to come into the arc of safety without an invitation will die. This is why I stay close to Jesus, making sure that my flesh dies daily. Everything I thought I was when I began this journey could not go with me into the Holy of Holies. It's there that I learned that this is not about me. This is about the Son of the living God. Without the knowledge of Jesus, I'm just a squatter.

The Lord spoke these words to me in my prayer closet: "I didn't write the script, so I can't change it." He said that all he needed me to do was play my part. He said it like this: "You know when you go to the movies and they show you the preview of something that's coming soon?" That means that the cast has already been picked out. All we're waiting on is the release date. He said, "Like natural like spiritual." From then on I understood that he was running the show. I am just a partner in his labor.

He is making sure that all things work together to fit into a plan and for those who love him and are called according to his design and purpose. God has a designer's plan for you. It will fit you perfectly.

I can remember when I first started learning about the Lord on my own and recognizing his voice for myself. He woke me up in the late midnight hour in March and said, "I want you to pray for Kevin Garnett." I did! When I finished, he asked me, "Do you know what they call him?"

I said, "Yes! The Big Ticket!"

He said, "That's you." He told me to turn on the TV. The Marcus and Joni Lamb show was airing. Dr. Mike Murdock was a guest. I had never seen them on television before. Mike Murdock began to say some things by the Holy Spirit. A powerful presence of the Lord appeared in my living room. From that day forward God was working on my faith. God wanted me to have the view of him that all things are possible with him.

That day my focus was on walking in the Spirit. I can see and hear in spirit. I have since then learned that God has no favorite. He does demonstrate his divine favor to those who believe him. I began to set my heart desires after God. Saying yes to God became easier. I became more conscious about God and less conscious about anything else. In my early stages of walking with God, I got offtrack. He was my spiritual mechanic. Anytime I got in the wrong lane, I went to him, and he put me back in the right lane. The Lord was anointing my strength so that I would make it through my pit on the way to my palace.

Father God, I come to you just as I am. Make me what you have predestined me to be. Cause every hindrance in my life that is keeping me from your all to come to an end right now.

Oftentimes we want to talk to God but we don't know how. We come to believe that asking someone else to pray to God for us will have a better impact than our talking to him ourselves. Now don't misunderstand; we should all pray for one another. But we must learn the benefits of a fellowship with God for ourselves. You don't have to count on the priest, preacher, mother, or father to talk to God. The way has been cleared for all to come boldly and make your request known to him. Who can better talk to God on your behalf than you? Speak to him from your heart. Tell him all. He knows all.

I believe God wants me to share with you. God wants to hear from you. I know your thoughts from afar. I also am longing to reveal to you the special assignment that I have for you. "Call unto me, and I will answer thee sayith the Lord, seek my face and I will reveal myself unto you. God wants to hear from me" (Jeremiah 33:3).

"Give thanks unto the Lord Almighty, for the Lord is good; for I will restore the fortunes of the land as they were before, says the Lord" (Jeremiah 33:11).

Lord, if I leave you, where would I go? If I leave you, whom would I find as good as you? To whom shall I go? You have eternal life. I believe, and I'm sure that you are Christ, so no place is safe outside of your will.

It's natural to have thoughts of leaving—just like in a natural relationship, especially when it seems like the wind just won't stop raging. Just know it won't rage forever. Whenever the Lord says "peace," there will be peace. There is a song called "My Soul Has Been Anchored in the Lord." Let that be your testimony.

We thank you, Lord, for being our umbrella in the rain. We thank you, Lord, for being our strength in the midst of the pain. We thank you for being our joy in the midst of all our sorrows, and we thank you, Lord, for being our shelter when we had no gain.

Celebration of Heart
May the song in your heart be a joyful one. As you celebrate another year of trusting and waiting on the Lord, may he light your way in the year to come. May you feel his presence forever near. Lord, hold us up and keep us safe. Let the joyful noise in our hearts continue to stay. Your strength, Lord, is our joy. We will continue to praise you and keep a heart of celebration.

He fashioned me for his glory! As I said, not my will but the Lord's will be done. He gave me a track record of victory! I became satisfied in Jesus. I received the peace of God, walking in divine authority. Jesus fully reinstated me to all of the benefits of salvation, love, and abundant living. He canceled every debt with his shed blood. I no longer have to practice sin. I have a choice. I choose not to. The power of his Holy Spirit and his Grace is what makes all of this possible. *Lord, we are available to you. Do what you want. Our storage is empty, and we are available to you. Amen.*

Here is a song I wrote for my husband-to-be:

> Never knew I had a chance at love. Really don't know how the outcome will turn. All I know is Jesus gave his word. He said if I trust in him I never can go wrong. Never knew a love could be so strong. Never knew I'd be the only one. All I know is Jesus gave his word. He said if I trust in him, this love could change the world. Never knew I had a chance at love. Really didn't know how the outcome would turn. All I know is Jesus gave his word. He said if I trust in him, the wait—it won't be long.

However, as the scripture says, "what no one ever saw or heard, what no one ever thought could happen, is the very thing God prepared for those who love him" (1 Corinthians 2:9).

FRIENDS QUOTES

Friends share and care. They learn to share your good and bad times. They understand that seasons must change.

Friends are selfless.

Friends are those you can count on to inspire you when no one else can or will. They will always do their best to try to encourage you.

Friends are joyous in your toughest times.

Friends are always there to tell you to keep going when everyone else is telling you to quit.

Friends love you at all times.

Friends stick around even when you encourage them to leave.

Friends believe you can and you will.

Friends encourage you to smile when you want to cry.

Friends tell you your only failure in life is deciding not to try again.

Friends are those who help you see what's inside of you.

Friends inspire the greatness in you.

Friends bring out the best in you.

Friends encourage you to do things you think you can't do.

Friends encourage you to reach for the impossible. You must always believe you have something to give.

Friends are your biggest cheerleaders even though they're on the sidelines.

Friends are considerate.

Friends are confident that helping you get there first is a great achievement.

Friends express their feelings to you when you are wrong. They know it's the healthiest thing for you and others.

Friends tell you that everything you need is already within you. All you have to do is tap into it.

Greater is he who is on the inside of you than any obstacle on the outside.

Friends call sometimes just to say, "I love you."

Friends stick close to you at all times. They don't run when your trouble double-teams you.

Friends understand the power in forgiving.

Friends understand how vital it is to forgive yourself and others to enjoy a healthy life. It's your ultimate pathway to achieving your goals in life.

Friends encourage you to forget those people, problems, and failures that should be behind you. Acknowledge what happened, and thank God. You are better and stronger. Be mindful that all the good and bad were needed in your life to push you to higher heights.

Friends encourage you to finish what you started even if the finish line looks too far away.

Friends remind you that no matter how bad you think your situation may be, others think theirs is worse. Your greatest days are still in front of you. Just keep the faith and keep running your race. The race is not given to the swift but to those who endure to the end.

Friends remind you that trouble doesn't last and the storm has to come to an end at some point. You will breathe again.

Friends remind you that this too shall pass. You don't have to pass out with it.

Friends remind you that in your darkest times you can find your greatest potential. You have hidden treasure on the inside.

Friends remind you that you can make a difference. You are the difference to someone somewhere, even when you don't believe you are. Someone is waiting to celebrate you and not just tolerate you.

Friends remind you that your very existence is a gift to you and the people around you. They truly do know and value your worth.

Friends remind you it's not what you say but how you say it. Remember to let your conversation match where you're going.

Friends remind you to always do unto others as you want them to do unto you. Remember that you just might be entertaining a messenger of God.

Friends remind you that even if everyone else walks out of your life, they haven't and never will. Focus on what you have instead of who's not there. Don't forget Jesus said he will never leave you or forsake you. If you left him, he's still right here with open arms to receive you back.

Friends are giving and not always taking.

Friends are not judgmental. They realize the power in being truthful to one another in love.

Friends are protective of one another's privacy.

Friends realize that you are capable of making your own decisions even when they don't think they are the right ones.

Friends realize that they can push you to grow from your mistakes.

Friends remind you that mistakes are all a part of this life. Your biggest mistake can be to believe that you won't make any.

Friends will share some of their mistakes with you if they believe that they can be helpful in preventing harmful or eternal damage to you and your loved ones. Try not to learn everything by experience. You can learn from others' mistakes. The Bible is a great place to learn.

Friends don't take sides.

Friends will let you know they're on your side if you need them.

Friends are valuable to each other.

Friends have your best interest at heart at all times.

If you bake a cake using a box cake mix, it takes only about thirty-five minutes to cook. But if you bake a 7 Up pound cake from scratch, it can take up to two hours to be done. It takes a little more time to bake a cake from scratch because of its ingredients. Think about that. Being patient produces the best results.

I'm going to keep my life in your hands. Every morning I awake, I'll give you praise. You've been my light through all the dark roads on which I have traveled. As I continue to walk my assigned journey, I'm going to keep my life in your hands. Jesus, keep my life in your hands. Your blood is why I'm not on sinking sand. I will taste all your goodness from your hands. God, your grace will lead me on to heaven. I'm going to keep my life in your hands. Every morning I awake, I'll give you praise.

Journal

Journal

Journal

Journal

Every scripture passage is inspired by God. All of them are useful for teaching, pointing out error, correcting people, and training them for a life that has God's approval !

2nd Timothy 3: 16

Thank you to all readers. Stay inspired!

ABOUT THE AUTHOR

Eboni is an upstanding young lady. She remains the same in every situation. She has played in TV shows that have shown her character. Eboni has also had the opportunity to speak to youth at public schools to let them know that no matter where they come from, God has the ultimate plan for all.

DEGREE

Doing
Everything
God
Requires
Everyday..Until
Eternity

Constitution rights: No one shall be subjected to arbitrary interference with his privacy, family, home or correspondence, nor the attacks upon his honour and reputation. Everyone has the right to the protection of law against such interference or attacks. Unfortunately, I went through all of these things. And is currently still going through them. And the law has part in my privacy interference. Though readers you might be thinking. How and why. I had these same thoughts. I left names unknown and a lot of details out of this book to avoid the possibility of law suits. And to protect people name and reputation. Though this was advised by Author House Lawyers. It caused rumors and lies against my name and the cause of writing this book. The cause of this book was and is to promote God's kingdom. So I had to give my history in order to give my testimony. Though most of the things I talked about was during my teenage years. The rumor attacks against my name was as if these things were current. So these updates and praise reports is to set the record straight.

Bible: Any story sounds true until someone tells the other side and sets the record straight

Bible: "Happy are you when people insult you and persecute you and tell all kinds of evil lies against you because you are my followers." Be happy and glad, this is how the prophets who lived before you were persecuted. Though these are the words of Jesus Christ. Nothing felt happy about the spreading of lies against my name. I can't fail to mention these things are spiritual: This song God used to remind me of his victory: Though: The enemy came up against my Name

The enemy came up against your character

You will win, win
You will win, win

The enemy came up against your health
The enemy came up against your finance
The enemy came up against your vision
The enemy came up against your business

You will win, win
You will win, win

I know you're hurt
I know you're torn. When you go through all of these things. The enemy doesn't want you to believe victory is possible. And in the natural it's not. So your mind has to be filled with God's word. You truly need Christ mind to prevail over Satan mind games. During my early part of serving Christ. I heard preachers say all you need is a word from the Lord. I've also heard, sometimes all God give you is a word. I found these statements to be true. This the word God gave through these rumors and lies:

Bible: Weapons made to attack you won't be successful; words spoken against you won't hurt at all. I, the LORD, promise to bless you with victory

When believers' faith has grown under the sound of God their not moved by feelings or sight. Their only moved by the word. And they only move when God speaks. Quote: God has countless of words in his vocabulary. Failure is not in there. Eboni King

Bible: Be assured that the testing of your faith [through experience] produces endurance [leading to spiritual maturity, and inner peace]. And let endurance have its perfect result *and* do a thorough work, so that you may be perfect and completely developed [in your faith], lacking in nothing. Experience is an important word in this scripture. It implies you must go through the testing of faith. Quote: Faith has no feelings: Eboni King

Quote: Your words are seeds. So whatever grows is what you planted. Eboni King

I never let up on sowing God's word through all of trials of testing of faith.

Bible: The Lord God has given Me (His Servant) the tongue of disciples [as One who is taught] That I may know how to sustain the weary with a word. He awakens Me morning by morning. He awakens My ear to listen as a disciple (as One who is taught). The Lord God has opened My ear and I have not been rebellious. Nor have I turned back. It's safe to say God pressured me into writing. He spoke several times to me and through others about I have an author on the inside of me. I couldn't see these things when God initially said it. Nor was my mind comprehending the magnitude of God's word. So I finally put something together in the title of My Change: Change Happens After Knowing God's Emotions. I thought God would be satisfied. I know how this sounds. But this was my initial mindset. I couldn't understand why God would want me to write about my unfortunate childhood life. Since it was full of sexual sins. I couldn't see how he could bring glory from it. So I was reluctant on sharing anything about my early life. So after my change had been out a while. I heard God speak a new title: I Changed My Mind (Subtitle: It's Not What You Think). I was working at Portillo during this time. I had intended on doing a series on my change. Though I had nothing in mind on when I would get around to it.

I had read Portillo story. About him having to change his name from the doghouse due to it belonging to someone else. And he could have a lawsuit against him. And this story was so inspiring. So I became excited about the new name God gave to replace my change. So I actually composed the manuscript of my change into I change my mind. So when my name went under attack with rumors and lies. I was confused. Because it was manuscript that had been published not long before. With a new title and additional manuscript. It seemed what I had worked so hard for. Was being tarnished with rumors and lies. Words are seeds. I got a call from a woman I considerate a true friend. She said; God said; tell you I had been lying on you all those years to my ex-husband. I asked; about what. She said; I was stealing thousands of dollars of his drug money. And was lying saying you was stealing it. I was numb. Considering there were current indirect lies and rumors against my name and book in regards to a man being murdered over owed drug money in a neighborhood where my mother resides. I was lost for words. All kinds of thoughts start swarming through my mind. Like no wonder he never liked me. And all those times I confronted you with it. You replied with, he thinks we bumping cats (lesbians). I would say, girl he doesn't know I'm strictly (penis). I used a different word when I was a sinner. I thought he must have thought you were playing the man role of the nonexistent bumping cats role. I guess because from time to time I would still be around after his money was stolen. He must have thought she didn't care about me stealing his money. Because of a relationship.

So I finally asked. Why were you stealing his money and blaming me? You didn't use drugs. She replied; shopping. I said it's not this much shopping in the world. Besides, you didn't buy expensive clothes. She really didn't have a logical answer. There isn't a logical answer. She said; she was a sinner. I was a sinner then, I didn't steal and I would have never lied on a friend. Definitely not to a man I'm in relationship with. And cause him to think negative about a person I hang with. She never considered these things. Not to mention. I didn't even know he was into the drug sales. I didn't believe in lying even as a sinner. Though I was dishonest with things pertaining to government funds during my sinner days. I was a person who spoke my mind. So there was not a lot of room for lying then. So these things were hurtful. I doubt if she realized the damaged this lie caused. To our friendship. And to the existing rumors and lies. I sold a book to a man I know of. And my ex knows more personally. To my knowledge he works and sells food. Not into any kind of drug sales. It has been rumor about his sexual preference. I do not know him like this. Nor what he likes or dislike. So since I been molested as a child orally by a female. I'm thankful. I've never had a sexual disorder. Nor a woman attraction. So my thoughts were. Whatever his sexual preference is. Salvation is administered in my book. Along with what I went through sexually. So perhaps these things can help those with like or similar situations. A relationship I had during my early adolescent years with a detective change my mindset about the drug sales. Officer Roberts had a tremendous impact on my decision to leave the neighborhood I was living in and the sales. Though this was unbeknownst to him during the time of the relationship. He knew I spent most of my time at the Casino Boats. He never would impose his opinions about what I should or shouldn't do. He would suggest things like investing into real estate as he was doing. He even offered to show me. Though I didn't consider the offer. I did appreciate the gesture. So when I gave my life to Christ Jesus drug sales or the thought was not a part of my life. So I couldn't believe these indirect lies and rumors were circulating. I say indirectly. Cause I've never been approached directly with the lies and rumors.

Quote: Truth shall outlast everyone lies. Eboni King

Bible: Hate evil, love good; maintain justice in the courtroom. If these things ever go to court. I'll be glad to state my innocence. The constitution says. Innocent until proven guilty. I been treated unruly by everyone as if I'm guilty over things I knew not of.

Bible: Evil people testify against me and accuse me of crimes I know nothing about

Journal

Journal

So I began noticing odd things regarding phone intrusion. I reported these things to the law. I didn't really know how to explain these things. I just knew people were on my phone listening to my conversations. When I would go about my normal day. I would hear conversations pertaining to things I had said in my privacy times. After I noticed these things were happening frequently. I knew my privacy had been stolen. I even went to the FBI facility to inquire about these things. I gave a name of a policeman my ex-husband knew with the possibility of his following by way of phone surveillance. They stated; I couldn't see why he or any authorities would be following you. I replied; I agree. I'm a published Author. I live holy unto Christ Jesus. And I respect the law and abiding citizens. And I should receive the same respect. So my determination increased to find out why was my phone under surveillance. I learned about prolific phone tracking devices. Such as cell phone trackers, commonly known as stingrays, has long been among law enforcements worst kept secrets, through the agency still refuses to acknowledge it. Stingrays are suitcase sized devices that can pinpoint a cellphone location within a few yards by posing as a cell tower. In the process, they also intercept information about other cellphones that happen to be near. A fact that has raised concerns among privacy advocates and some lawmakers. These devices are now being used among citizens. And I have been victimized by these devices and along with other devices. And I haven't had any privacy in years.

In 2012 I started an online (Facebook) relationship with gospel singer, Marvin Sapp. I was helping him spiritually with the word of God during the worst trials of his life. I gave him spiritual counsel and direction through the word of God. And the leading of the Holy Spirit. Then shortly afterwards I noticed a physical attraction on his part. I then stated, I thought it was too soon for him to be thinking about dating. I said considering the circumstances he should give it at least two years before he thinks of dating. Not too long after, he started a posting: To my future from me. I told him to let the rivers flow. These posting was then composed into a book. The courting relationship started somewhere along these lines. Things were going good. I was speaking prophetically things into his life and God was manifesting these things. I was so into him during these times. I didn't know much about love in a relationship. Nor what people mean when they say I'm in love with you. These things were foreign to me. I knew God's love from my personal relationship with Jesus Christ. So I knew how to love. I felt he needed love from a genuine heart. So I remember direct messaging: I love all of you. I'm spiritual and visual. And I knew with everything he was going through including weight fluctuations. He needed to hear this. And I meant it. I never say anything unless I mean it. So many interferences happen during this time. I care not to talk about at this time. So I asked him did he still want the relationship. He and I vowed to. He couldn't seem to answer appropriately or in a timely manner. So I left the relationship.

Quote: It's important to define every stage of the relationship. Eboni King

Quote: A relationship undefined could mean there's possibly room for someone else: Eboni King
Then I began a relationship with Mogul Media Movie Producer Tyler Perry. He and I became close friends by way of Marvin and I relationship socially towards the end of 2012. Then a love relationship started towards the end of 2013. This phone relationship lasted up until the end of 2019. I ended it after a drive to Atlanta at his discretion to come. And he didn't come down to meet at my arrival at his studio. And know this was not some catfish ploy. I know them spiritually and socially. And they know me socially. It's much more to it than this. So these social relationships seem to be the primary cause of my privacy

being stolen. And is now a part of the whole country everyday life. Everyone seems to get a kick out of following me through this unlawful phone tracking. Though Tyler Perry tried to alert me to these phone invasions and let's blameitonkway. I had no idea what he was saying. I learned these things spiritually afterwards. I'll elaborate on these things during other books, etc.

Bible: My protection and success come from God alone. He is my refuge, a Rock where no enemy can reach me. O servants of Christ, trust him all the time. Pour out your longings before him, for he can help. The greatest of men or the lowest - both alike are nothing in his sight. They weigh less than air on scales. I've certainly had to rely on this scripture during this viral theft of my privacy. Bible: God is my rock and salvation; my fortress and my defense, I will not be shaken or discouraged. I have gone through a lot of test and trials. These 16 plus years I been serving Christ Jesus without fail. Quote: Standing on Christ you can't fall. And in him you won't fail: Eboni King God continued to give me his word and quotes through these unfortunate circumstances. Though the privacy theft affected my finances, business endeavors, health (hair loss due to these stressful privacy thefts), jobs (nitpickers) etc. God kept my mind in his perfect peace. This is why God is worthy of my praise of right living according to biblical standards.

God has spoken once, twice have I heard this: THAT POWER BELONGS TO GOD. So though these people under the influence of Satan tried everything they could to hinder me from doing what God created and chosen me to do. All their plots failed. My lifestyle in Christ or prayer life didn't falter. Nor could anything Satan do interfere

Quote: Your language of prayer says to your circumstances. I don't have to go through this alone. Eboni King

Whatever trial is not God sent. He can still use it for his glory.

Quote: Sometimes success is just simply not giving up. Eboni King
Bible: Also to You, O Lord, belong loving kindness and compassion, For you compensate every man according to (the value of) his work.

Bible: For we speak as messengers from God, trusted by him to tell the truth; we change his message not one bit to suit the taste of those who hear it; for we serve God alone, who examines our hearts' deepest thoughts. I stayed true to the gospel of Jesus Christ in word and my lifestyle through all of these things. I'm happy to say 3/13/2006 I'm still celibate (no sex until marriage) God's way. And considering sex before I was even a teenager. This is God's miraculous power of his word. I didn't grow up on the word of God. Nor did I have a sex education class. Nor talks about save yourself for marriage. My parents weren't claimants of Christ Jesus. My mother has some religious beliefs. And my father never talked any beliefs of religion. Though he had a Koran book around. I never seen him read it. Nor did he impose any religion in the household. They used drugs most of their lives. And I'm happy to say my father life ended drug free. And he asks my mom to promise him she would discontinue her drug usage. Though it was shortly after. I'm happy to say my mom has been drug free since. She didn't go to a drug rehabilitation center. She wasn't claiming Christ. She gave it up on a promise word. And she hasn't had a thought nor desire. It's been a decade.

Freedom from addictions is in your mind. When you make the decision to give it up.

And if your claiming Christ Jesus it's nothing God's power can't free you from.

Quote: Murmuring can distort your vision: Eboni King

Quote: Never become mentally involved with the trials of life. It's not a permanent thing: Eboni King

Quote: God determines the length of believers trials. They won't last longer than the ability to handle them: Eboni King

Quote: Praise lifts the weight of a trial: Eboni King

Quote: If you want some relief from the sound of Satan. Start dancing: Eboni King

Quote: Illusions never turn into something real. Never let fear intimidate you: Eboni King

Quote: The brightness of God's glory always come after the depth of a storm: Eboni King

Bible: People with their minds set on you, you keep completely whole, Steady on their feet, because they keep at it and don't quit

Quote: God's peace is the answer for a healthy mind: Eboni King

Printed in the United States
by Baker & Taylor Publisher Services